I0410008

U.S. ENVIRONMENTAL PROTECTION AGENCY
OFFICE OF INSPECTOR GENERAL

Catalyst for Improving the Environment

Audit Report

Fiscal Year 2010 and 2009 Financial Statements for the Pesticide Registration Fund

Report No. 11-1-0157

March 10, 2011

Report Contributors:

Paul Curtis
Robert Smith
Bill Samuel
Catherine Allen
Sabrina Berry
Guillermo Mejia
Javier Negron
Demetrios Papakonstantinou
Myka Sparrow
Lynda Taylor

Abbreviations

CSRS	Civil Service Retirement System
EPA	U.S. Environmental Protection Agency
FERS	Federal Employees Retirement System
FMFIA	Federal Managers' Financial Integrity Act
FY	Fiscal year
OCFO	Office of the Chief Financial Officer
OIG	Office of Inspector General
OMB	Office of Management and Budget
OPM	Office of Personnel Management
PRIA	Pesticide Registration Improvement Act

At a Glance

Catalyst for Improving the Environment

Why We Did This Audit

The Pesticide Registration Improvement Act (PRIA) requires that we perform an annual audit of the Pesticide Registration Fund (known as the PRIA Fund) financial statements.

Background

To expedite the registration of certain pesticides, Congress authorized the U.S. Environmental Protection Agency (EPA) to assess and collect pesticide registration fees. The fees collected are deposited into the PRIA Fund. The Agency is required to prepare financial statements that present financial information about the PRIA Fund. PRIA also requires the establishment of decision time review periods for pesticide registration actions, and requires the Office of Inspector General to perform an analysis of the Agency's compliance with those review periods.

For further information, contact our Office of Congressional, Public Affairs and Management at (202) 566-2391.

The full report is at:
www.epa.gov/oig/reports/2011/
20110310-11-1-0157.pdf

Fiscal Year 2010 and 2009 Financial Statements for the Pesticide Registration Fund

Opinion

We rendered an unqualified, or clean, opinion on EPA's Pesticide Registration Fund financial statements for fiscal years 2010 and 2009, meaning that they were fairly presented and free of material misstatement.

Internal Control Significant Deficiency Noted

We noted one significant deficiency in internal controls. EPA misapplied federal retirement benefit cost factors in calculating fiscal year 2010 imputed cost related to the Civil Service Retirement System and the Federal Employees Retirement System. Imputed costs are costs that are not fully reimbursed. This significant deficiency resulted in an understatement of $120,422. The Agency has corrected fiscal year 2010 imputed costs in the PRIA Fund financial statements.

Compliance with Decision Time Review Periods

The Agency was in substantial compliance with the statutory decision time frames.

Agency Comments and Office of Inspector General Evaluation

The Office of the Chief Financial Officer and the Office of Chemical Safety and Pollution Prevention concurred with our general conclusions that the financial statements are fairly presented and free of material misstatements.

UNITED STATES ENVIRONMENTAL PROTECTION AGENCY
WASHINGTON, D.C. 20460

March 10, 2011

MEMORANDUM

SUBJECT: Fiscal Year 2010 and 2009 Financial Statements for the
Pesticide Registration Fund
Report No. 11-1-0157

FROM: Arthur A. Elkins, Jr.
Inspector General

TO: Steve Owens
Assistant Administrator for Chemical Safety and Pollution Prevention

Barbara Bennett
Chief Financial Officer

This is our report on the audit of the U.S. Environmental Protection Agency's (EPA's) Fiscal Year 2010 and 2009 Financial Statements for the Pesticide Registration Fund, conducted by the EPA Office of Inspector General (OIG). This report represents the opinion of the OIG and does not necessarily represent the final EPA position. Final determination on matters in this report will be made by EPA managers in accordance with established audit resolution procedures.

The estimated direct labor and travel costs for this report are $83,785.

Action Required

Because this report contains no recommendations, you are not required to respond to this report. We have no objections to the further release of this report to the public. This report will be available at http://www.epa.gov/oig.

If you or your staff have any questions regarding this report, please contact Melissa Heist at 202-566-0899 or Heist.Melissa@epa.gov, Paul Curtis at (202) 566-2523 or Curtis.Paul@epa.gov, or Robert Smith at (202) 566-2531 or Smith.RobertL@epa.gov.

Table of Contents

Inspector General's Report on the Fiscal Year 2010 and 2009 Financial Statements for the Pesticide Registration Fund

Attachments

Appendices

Inspector General's Report on the Fiscal Year 2010 and 2009 Financial Statements for the Pesticide Registration Fund

The Administrator
U.S. Environmental Protection Agency

We have audited the Pesticide Registration Fund (known as the PRIA Fund) balance sheet as of September 30, 2010, and 2009, and the related statements of net cost, changes in net position, and budgetary resources for the years then ended. These financial statements are the responsibility of U.S. Environmental Protection Agency (EPA) management. Our responsibility is to express an opinion on these financial statements based upon our audit.

We conducted our audit in accordance with generally accepted government auditing standards; the standards applicable to financial statements contained in *Government Auditing Standards,* issued by the Comptroller General of the United States; and Office of Management and Budget (OMB) Bulletin No. 07-04, *Audit Requirements for Federal Financial Statements, as Amended.* These standards require that we plan and perform the audit to obtain reasonable assurance as to whether the financial statements are free of material misstatements. An audit includes examining, on a test basis, evidence supporting the amounts and disclosures in the financial statements. An audit also includes assessing the accounting principles used and significant estimates made by management, as well as evaluating the overall financial statement presentation. We believe that our audit provides a reasonable basis for our opinion.

In our opinion, the financial statements, including the accompanying notes, present fairly, in all material respects, the assets, liabilities, net position, net cost, changes in net position, and budgetary resources of the PRIA Fund, as of and for the years ended September 30, 2010, and 2009, in conformity with accounting principles generally accepted in the United States of America.

Evaluation of Internal Controls

As defined by OMB, internal control, as it relates to the financial statements, is a process, affected by the Agency's management and other personnel, designed to provide reasonable assurance that the following objectives are met:

Reliability of financial reporting—Transactions are properly recorded, processed, and summarized to permit the preparation of the financial statements in accordance with generally accepted accounting principles; and assets are safeguarded against loss from unauthorized acquisition, use, or disposition.

Compliance with applicable laws, regulations, and government-wide policies— Transactions are executed in accordance with laws governing the use of budget authority, government-wide policies, laws identified by OMB, and other laws and regulations that could have a direct and material effect on the financial statements.

In planning and performing our audit, we considered EPA's internal controls over Pesticide Registration Improvement Act (PRIA) financial reporting by obtaining an understanding of the Agency's internal controls, determining whether internal controls have been placed in operation, assessing control risk, and performing tests of controls. We did this as a basis for designing our auditing procedures for the purpose of expressing an opinion on the financial statements and to comply with OMB audit guidance, not to express an opinion on internal control. Accordingly, we do not express an opinion on internal control over financial reporting. We limited our internal control testing to those controls necessary to achieve the objectives described in OMB Bulletin No. 07-04, *Audit Requirements for Federal Financial Statements, as Amended.* We did not test all internal controls relevant to operating objectives as broadly defined by the Federal Managers' Financial Integrity Act (FMFIA), such as those controls relevant to ensuring efficient operations. The objective of our audit was not to provide assurance on internal controls and, accordingly, we do not express an opinion on internal controls.

Our consideration of the internal controls over financial reporting would not necessarily disclose all matters in the internal control over financial reporting that might be significant deficiencies. Under standards issued by the American Institute of Certified Public Accountants, a significant deficiency is a deficiency, or combination of deficiencies, in internal control that is less severe than a material weakness, yet important enough to merit attention by those charged with governance. A material weakness is a deficiency, or combination of deficiencies, in internal controls, such that there is a reasonable possibility that a material misstatement of the entity's financial statements will not be prevented, or detected and corrected on a timely basis. Because of inherent limitations in any internal controls, misstatements, losses, or noncompliance may nevertheless occur and not be detected. We noted a certain matter involving the internal controls and its operations that we considered to be a significant deficiency. We do not consider this matter to be a material weakness.

Significant Deficiency: Incorrect Cost Factors Were Used to Compute Imputed Costs

EPA misapplied federal retirement benefit cost factors in calculating fiscal year (FY) 2010 imputed cost related to the Civil Service Retirement System (CSRS) and the Federal Employees Retirement System (FERS). In August 2010, the Office of Personnel Management (OPM) issued Benefits Administration Letter, Number: 10-306, which provided FY 2010 retirement cost factors that should be applied in FY 2010 year-end financial reporting. EPA did not exercise due care in computing FY 2010 imputed costs and inadvertently used the FY 2009 retirement cost factors. This error resulted in a significant understatement for the PRIA Fund in the amount of $120,422. After we brought the issue to the attention of the Office of the Chief Financial Officer, that office made the appropriate adjustment for the FY 2010 cost factors.

Comparison of EPA's FMFIA Report with Our Evaluation of Internal Controls

OMB Bulletin No. 07-04, *Audit Requirements for Federal Financial Statements, as Amended,* requires us to compare material weaknesses disclosed during the audit with those material weaknesses reported in the Agency's FMFIA report that relate to the financial statements and identify material weaknesses disclosed by the audit that were not reported in the Agency's FMFIA report.

For financial statement audit and financial reporting purposes, OMB defines a material weakness in internal control as a deficiency or combination of deficiencies in internal control, such that there is a reasonable possibility that a material misstatement of the financial statements will not be prevented or detected and corrected on a timely basis. The Agency did not report, and our audit did not detect, any material weaknesses for FY 2010 impacting the PRIA Fund.

Tests of Compliance With Laws and Regulations

In accordance with PRIA, the Administrator is required to publish a schedule of decision time review periods for pesticide registration actions and corresponding registration fees in the Federal Register. Decision time review periods are specified time limits for the Agency to grant or deny pesticide registrations. PRIA also requires the Office of Inspector General (OIG) to perform an analysis of the Agency's compliance with decision time review periods. The Agency was in substantial compliance with the statutory decision time frames.

As part of obtaining reasonable assurance as to whether the financial statements are free of material misstatement, we tested compliance with those laws and regulations that could either materially affect the PRIA financial statements, or that we considered significant to the audit. The objective of our audit, including our tests of compliance with applicable laws and regulations, was not to provide an opinion on overall compliance with such provisions. Accordingly, we do not express such an opinion. We did not identify any noncompliances that would result in a material misstatement to the audited financial statements.

Management's Discussion and Analysis Section of the Financial Statements

Our audit work related to the information presented in the Management's Discussion and Analysis of the Pesticide Program included comparing the overview information with information in the principal financial statements for consistency. We did not identify material inconsistencies between the information presented in the two documents.

Prior Audit Coverage

In FY 2009, we did not identify any significant deficiencies affecting the PRIA Fund. During previous financial or financial-related audits, we reported a significant deficiency because we could not assess the adequacy of Integrated Financial Management System automated controls.

EPA has taken additional steps to correct the significant deficiency related to its financial system by undertaking a project to replace its core financial application. The new EPA Financial System is anticipated to go live in October 2012. We will continue to report a significant deficiency concerning our inability to test application controls due to insufficient system documentation until the new system is implemented. (*Audit of EPA's Fiscal 2010 and 2009 Consolidated Financial Statements*, Report No. 11-1-0015, issued November 15, 2010)

Noteworthy Achievements

The Office of Pesticide Programs has done a commendable job in complying with statutory decision time review periods for pesticide registration actions. During our sample testing, we found that the Agency had completed the PRIA decisions due during FY 2010 within the statutory time frames.

Agency Comments and OIG Evaluation

The Office of the Chief Financial Officer and the Office of Chemical Safety and Pollution Prevention concurred with our general conclusions that the financial statements are fairly presented and free of material misstatements. Their response was submitted in an e-mail and is not included as an attachment to this report.

Paul C. Curtis
Director, Financial Statement Audits
Office of Inspector General
U.S. Environmental Protection Agency
March xx, 2011

Significant Deficiency

Table of Contents

Incorrect Cost Factors Were Used to Compute Imputed Costs

EPA misapplied federal retirement benefit cost factors in calculating FY 2010 imputed cost related to CSRS and FERS. In August 2010, OPM issued Benefits Administration Letter, Number: 10-306, which provided FY 2010 retirement cost factors that should be applied in FY 2010 year-end financial reporting. EPA did not exercise due care in computing FY 2010 imputed costs and inadvertently used the FY 2009 retirement cost factors. This error resulted in a significant understatement for the PRIA Fund in the amount of $120,422.

Imputed costs related to pensions are the difference between pension service cost and the employees' and federal pension contributions. The pension service cost is determined by multiplying the basic pay paid to employees for each CSRS and FERS category by the applicable cost factors. The FY 2010 cost factor for most CSRS-covered employees was 30.1 percent and for most FERS-covered employees was 13.8 percent. For FY 2009, these amounts were 25.8 percent and 12.3 percent, respectively.

The Office of the Chief Financial Officer (OCFO) has quality control procedures in place that should have prevented this error; however, in this instance, the control procedures were not effective. We identified this discrepancy during our audit of EPA's FY 2010 financial statements and informed OCFO of the error in November 2010. OCFO did not consider the impact of this error before issuing the draft PRIA financial statements. After we brought this issue to the attention of OCFO, that office made the appropriate adjustment for the FY 2010 cost factors. Accordingly, we have no recommendations.

Status of Recommendations and Potential Monetary Benefits

		RECOMMENDATIONS				POTENTIAL MONETARY BENEFITS (in $000s)	
Rec. No.	Page No.	Subject	Status[1]	Action Official	Planned Completion Date	Claimed Amount	Agreed To Amount
		No recommendations					

FYs 2010 and 2009 PESTICIDE REGISTRATION FUND (PRIA) FINANCIAL STATEMENTS

Produced by the U.S. Environmental Protection Agency
Office of the Chief Financial Officer
Office of Financial Management

TABLE OF CONTENTS

Management's Discussion and Analysis

MANAGEMENT'S DISCUSSION AND ANALYSIS

The Agency's Office of Pesticide Programs (OPP) was established to administer the Federal Insecticide, Fungicide and Rodenticide Act (FIFRA) to protect public health and the environment. The law requires the Agency to balance public health and environmental concerns with the expected economic benefits derived from pesticides. The guiding principles of the pesticide program are to reduce risks from pesticides in food, the workplace, and other exposure pathways and to prevent pollution by encouraging the use of new and safer pesticides.

With passage of the Pesticide Registration Improvement Act (PRIA) of 2003, the pesticide program now administers the Pesticide Registration Fund. PRIA authorizes the collection of new fees for pesticide registrations. Registration service fees are deposited into the Registration Fund and made available for obligation to the extent provided in appropriation Acts, and are available without fiscal year limitation.

Pesticide Registration

Under the authority of FIFRA and the Federal Food, Drug, and Cosmetic Act (FFDCA) as amended by the Food Quality Protection Act (FQPA), no person or State can distribute or sell any pesticide that is not registered with the Agency. The pesticide registration program works to decrease the risk to the public from pesticide use through the regulatory review of new pesticides. In 2004, Congress passed PRIA, with deadlines for completion of certain registration actions. As part of the registration program, EPA expedites the registration of reduced-risk pesticide uses, which are generally presumed to pose lower risks to consumers, workers, groundwater, and/or wildlife. These accelerated pesticide reviews provide an incentive for industry to develop, register, and use lower risk pesticides. Additionally, the availability of these reduced-risk pesticides provides alternatives to older, potentially more harmful products currently on the market.

Biological agents are potential weapons that could be exploited by terrorists against the United States. EPA's pesticides antimicrobial program is working to help address this threat. Antimicrobials play an important role in public health and safety. EPA is conducting comprehensive scientific assessments and developing test protocols to determine the safety and efficacy of products used against chemical and biological weapons of mass destruction, and registering products as necessary. EPA is also developing a timeline for prioritizing and implementing the tests. In addition, the Section 18 program provides emergency exemption to any part of FIFRA. This authority is typically used by States on an emergency basis. EPA has recently used this authority to help with homeland security. Section 18 exemptions have been authorized to help with anthrax and soybean rust.

PRIA established registration service fees for certain antimicrobials, biopesticides and conventional pesticides registration actions. The category of action, the amount of the registration service fee, and the corresponding decision review periods by year are prescribed in the statute. The goal is to create a more predictable evaluation process for affected pesticide decisions, and couple the collection of individual fees with specific decision review periods. The legislation also promotes shorter decision review periods for reduced-risk applications. PRIA became effective on March 23, 2004, and the collection of registration fees were authorized through FY 2008. PRIA was reauthorized with passage of the Pesticide Registration Improvement Renewal Act (commonly referred to as PRIA 2) on October 9, 2007. PRIA 2 became effective retroactive to October 1, 2007, and the collection of registration fees are now authorized through FY 2012. In order to help ensure a smooth transition (if PRIA 2 is not re-authorized), PRIA 2 reduces the registration service fees by 40 percent in FY 2013 and then by 70 percent in FY 2014. For any application received after September 30, 2012, but before September 30, 2014, the reduced registration service fee applies, while the decision review periods do not.

In order for a pending or a new application covered by PRIA to be deemed complete and subject to the decision review periods, a registrant is required to pay the applicable fee or receive a waiver from the fees[1]. For most applications, the decision review period starts 21 days after submission of the application - provided that the fee has been paid, fee waiver granted or in the case of a 75% or 50% fee waiver under PRIA 2, the fee has been paid and waiver granted. The legislation provides fee waivers for certain categories of small businesses, and minor uses[2]. Exemptions from the requirement to pay a registration service fee is provided under PRIA 2 for applications solely associated with IR-4 petitions[3]. Applications from federal and state agencies are also exempt from registration service fees. If the registrant requests a waiver or reduction of the fee, the decision review period will begin when the Agency grants such request or in the case of small business fee waivers, no more than 60 days after receipt of the waiver application. If it is determined that a fee is required and thus the waiver is not granted, the decision review period starts after the fee is collected.

Applications received prior to October 1, 2007 are covered by PRIA 1. Applications received in FY08 are covered by PRIA 2 and PRIA 2 contains the same audit provision as PRIA 1. PRIA 2 imposed minimum payment requirements; requires the EPA to reject an application

---

[1] Out of approximately 9949 completed PRIA actions since the start of PRIA, more than 99% were completed on or before the PRIA/PRIA 2 due date.

[2] Minor use pesticides are those that produce relatively little revenue for their manufacturers, for a variety of reasons. They may be registered for a seldom seen pest, or for a crop that is not grown by a large number of producers. However, minor crops include some high revenue fruit, vegetable, and ornamental crops.
[3] The IR-4 (Interregional Research Project No.4) program is involved in making sure that pesticides are registered for use on minor crops. IR-4 helps by conducting research on minor use pesticides, pesticides that would not otherwise be profitable to manufacture.

for an unpaid fee; provides the ability to reject an application if it fails an initial content screen and retain a portion of the fee; increased the fee categories or types of applications covered by PRIA from 90 to 140; allows the use of investment income; eliminated the 100% fee waiver for small businesses; and increased the amount to support worker protection activities.

Research Program Description

EPA's pesticides and toxics research program continues to examine risks resulting from exposure to pesticides and toxic chemicals. The research is designed to support the Agency's efforts to reduce current and future risks to the environment and to humans by preventing and/or controlling the production of new chemicals and products of biotechnology that pose unreasonable risk, as well as assessing and reducing the risks of chemicals and products of biotechnology already in commerce. The research program's major goals are: (1) to provide predictive tools to prioritize testing requirements; enhance interpretation of data to improve human health and ecological risk assessments; and inform decision-making regarding high priority pesticides and toxic substances; (2) to develop probabilistic risk assessments to protect natural populations of birds, fish, other wildlife, and non-target plants; and (3) to provide the tools necessary to make decisions related to products of biotechnology.

In providing research on methods, models, and data to support decision-making regarding specific individual or classes of pesticides and toxic substances that are of high priority, the program is developing:
- Predictive biomarkers, quantitative structure activity relationships, and alternative test methods for prioritizing and screening chemicals for a number of adverse effects (e.g., neurotoxicity, reproductive toxicity) that will lead to a reduction in and more efficient use of whole animals in toxicity testing; and
- Data and protocols on the impact of waste water treatment technologies on pesticides and their products of transformation.

To support the development of probabilistic risk assessments to protect endangered populations of birds, fish, other wildlife, and non-target plants from pesticides while making sure farmers and communities have the pest control tools they need, this program has four key research components:
- Extrapolation among wildlife species and exposure scenarios of concern;
- Population biology to improve population dynamics in spatially-explicit habitats;
- Models for assessing the relative risk of chemical and non-chemical stressors; and
- Models to define geographical regional/spatial scales for risk assessment.

Methods for characterization of population-level risks of toxic substances to aquatic life and wildlife also are being developed as part of the Agency's long-term goal of developing scientifically valid approaches for assessing spatially-explicit, population-level risks to wildlife populations and non-target plants and plant communities from pesticides, toxic chemicals and multiple stressors while advancing the development of probabilistic risk assessment.

Additionally, research to support decision-making related to products of biotechnology includes:

- Development of methods to assess the potential allergenicity of genetically engineered plants.
- Characterization of the environmental impact of genetically engineered plants and developing methods to reduce them.

Enforcement and Compliance Assurance Program Description

The Pesticide Enforcement and Compliance Assurance Program focuses on pesticide product and user compliance. These include problems relating to pesticide worker safety, certification and training of applicators, ineffective antimicrobial products, food safety, adverse effects, risks of pesticides to endangered species, pesticide containers and containment facilities, and e-commerce and misuse. The enforcement and compliance assurance program provides compliance assistance to the regulated community through its National Agriculture Compliance Assistance Center, seminars, guidance documents, brochures, and other forms of communication to ensure knowledge of and compliance with environmental laws.

EPA's grant support to states' and tribes' pesticide programs emphasizes its commitment to maintaining a strong compliance and enforcement presence. Agency Cooperative Agreement priorities for FY2008 - FY2010 include the enforcement of worker protection standards; compliance monitoring and enforcement activities related to the newly promulgated pesticide container and containment rules, and program performance reporting. Core program activities include inspections of producing establishments; dealers/distributors/retailers; e-commerce; imports and exports, and pesticide misuse. Additionally, through the Cooperative Agreement resources we support inspector training and training for state/tribal senior managers, scientists, and supervisors.

Highlights and Accomplishments

Registration Financial Perspective

During FY 2010, the Agency's obligations charged against the Pesticide Registration Fund for the cost of registration were $18.1 million and 69.2 workyears (all obligated by OPP).

Appropriated funds are used in addition to Registration funds. In FY 2010, the enacted operating plan included approximately $39.1 million in appropriated funds for registration activities. The unobligated balance in the Fund at the end of FY 2010 was $7.4 million.

The Fund has two types of receipts: fee collections and interest earned on investments. Of the $18.6 million in FY 2010 receipts, more than 99.9% were fee collections.

Registration Program Performance Measures

The following measures support the program's strategic goals of Healthy Communities and Ecosystems as contained in the FY 2010 President's budget.

Measure 1: Number of new active ingredients registered.

Results: In FY 2010, EPA registered 22 new active ingredients, of which 17 are biopesticides, and 4 are conventional pesticides with domestic uses. This measure includes both reduced-risk and non-reduced-risk pesticides.

Measure 2: Progress in Registering Reduced-risk Pesticides.

Results: In FY 2010, EPA registered 18 reduced-risk new active ingredients, of which 17 were biological pesticides and 1 was a conventional pesticide. Biological pesticides are certain types of pesticides derived from such natural materials as animals, plants, bacteria, and certain minerals. They are usually less toxic and are typically considered safer pesticides than the traditional conventional chemicals; therefore, the 17 biopesticides new active ingredients are counted as reduced-risk pesticides. Conventional "reduced risk" pesticides have one or more of the following advantages over currently registered pesticides: low impact on human health, low toxicity to non-target organisms, low potential for groundwater contamination, lower use rates, low pest resistance potential, and compatibility with integrated pest management strategies.

Measure 3: Number of New Food Uses Registered.

Results: EPA registered 242 new food uses for previously registered active ingredients. Of these new uses, 233 were for conventional pesticides, 2 were for antimicrobial pesticides, and 7 were for biopesticides.

Measure 4: Progress in Registering Reduced-risk New Uses.

Results: Included in the new uses registered are 25 reduced-risk.

PRINCIPAL
FINANCIAL STATEMENTS

TABLE OF CONTENTS

Financial Statements

Notes to Financial Statements

Environmental Protection Agency
PRIA
Balance Sheet
For the Years Ended September 30, 2010 and 2009
(Dollars in Thousands)

	FY 2010	FY 2009
ASSETS		
Intragovernmental:		
Fund Balance With Treasury (Note 2)	$ 15,094	$ 15,140
Other (Note 3)	100	-
Total Intragovernmental	$ 15,194	$ 15,140
Accounts Receivable, Net	2	-
Property, Plant & Equipment, Net (Note 4)	4,445	3,644
Total Assets	$ **19,641**	$ **18,784**
LIABILITIES		
Intragovernmental:		
Accounts Payable and Accrued Liabilities	141	202
Other (Note 5)	21	79
Total Intragovernmental	$ 162	$ 281
Accounts Payable & Accrued Liabilities	$ 1,088	$ 1,320
Payroll & Benefits Payable (Note 6)	239	956
Other (Note 5)	14,088	13,421
Total Liabilities	$ 15,577	$ 15,978
NET POSITION		
Cumulative Results of Operations	4,064	2,806
Total Net Position	4,064	2,806
Total Liabilities and Net Position	$ **19,641**	$ **18,784**

The accompanying notes are an integral part of these statements.

Environmental Protection Agency
PRIA
Statement of Net Cost
For the Years Ended September 30, 2010 and 2009
(Dollars in Thousands)

	FY 2010	FY 2009
COSTS		
Gross Costs (Note 9)	$ 16,990	$ 16,314
Expenses from Other Appropriations (Note 7)	37,256	49,215
Total Costs	$ 54,246	$ 65,529
Less:		
Earned Revenue (Notes 8 and 9)	17,885	17,850
NET COST OF OPERATIONS (Note 9)	$ 36,361	$ 47,679

The accompanying notes are an integral part of these statements.

Environmental Protection Agency
PRIA
Statement of Changes in Net Position
For the Years Ended September 30, 2010 and 2009
(Dollars in Thousands)

		FY 2010		FY 2009
Cumulative Results of Operations:				
Net Position - Beginning of Period		2,806		1,249
Beginning Balances, as Adjusted	$	2,806	$	1,249
Budgetary Financing Sources:				
Nonexchange Revenue - Securities Investment		6		8
Nonexchange Revenue - Other		2		-
Income from Other Appropriations (Note 7)		37,256		49,215
Total Budgetary Financing Sources	$	37,264	$	49,223
Other Financing Sources (Non-Exchange)				
Imputed Financing Sources		355		13
Total Other Financing Sources	$	355	$	13
Net Cost of Operations		(36,361)		(47,679)
Net Change		1,258		1,557
Cumulative Results of Operations	$	4,064	$	2,806

The accompanying notes are an integral part of these statements.
Environmental Protection Agency

PRIA
Statement of Budgetary Resources
For the Years Ended September 30, 2010 and 2009
(Dollars in Thousands)

		FY 2010		FY 2009
BUDGETARY RESOURCES				
Unobligated Balance, Brought Forward, October 1:	$	6,980	$	8,872
Adjusted Subtotal		6,980		8,872
Recoveries of Prior Year Unpaid Obligations		-		319
Budgetary Authority:				
Appropriation		18,557		15,998
Spending Authority from Offsetting Collections				
Earned:				
Collected		3		2
Total Spending Authority from Offsetting Collections		3		2
Total Budgetary Resources	$	25,540	$	25,191
STATUS OF BUDGETARY RESOURCES				
Obligations Incurred:				
Direct	$	18,147	$	18,211
Total Obligations Incurred		18,147		18,211
Unobligated Balances:				
Apportioned		7,368		6,980
Total Unobligated Balances		7,368		6,980
Unobligated Balances Not Available		25		-
Total Status of Budgetary Resources	$	25,540	$	25,191

		FY 2010		FY 2009
CHANGE IN OBLIGATED BALANCE				
Obligated Balance, Net:				
Unpaid Obligations, Brought Forward, October 1	$	8,161	$	7,812
Total Unpaid Obligated Balance, Net		8,161		7,812
Obligations Incurred, Net		18,147		18,211
Less: Gross Outlays		(18,607)		(17,543)
Less: Recoveries of Prior Year Unpaid Obligations, Actual		-		(319)
Total, Change in Obligated Balance		7,701		8,161
Obligated Balance, Net, End of Period:				
Unpaid Obligations		7,701		8,161
Total, Unpaid Obligated Balance, Net, End of Period	$	7,701	$	8,161
NET OUTLAYS				
Net Outlays:				
Gross Outlays	$	18,607	$	17,543
Less: Offsetting Collections		(3)		(2)
Less: Distributed Offsetting Receipts (Note 1 Section L)		(18,557)		(15,833)
Total, Net Outlays	$	47	$	1,708

The accompanying notes are an integral part of these statements.

Environmental Protection Agency
PRIA
Notes to Financial Statements
(Dollars in Thousands)

Note 1. ***Summary of Significant Accounting Policies***

A. Reporting Entity

The U.S. Environmental Protection Agency (EPA or the Agency) was created in 1970 by executive reorganization from various components of other Federal agencies in order to better marshal and coordinate federal pollution control efforts. The Agency is generally organized around the media and substances it regulates -- air, water, land, hazardous waste, pesticides and toxic substances.

The Pesticide Registration Fund (PRIA) is authorized under the Pesticide Registration Improvement Act of 2003 (which amended the Federal Insecticide, Fungicide, and Rodenticide Act -- FIFRA), and became effective on March 23, 2004. This Act authorizes EPA to assess and collect pesticide registration service fees on applications submitted to register pesticides covered by this Act, as well as, assess and collect fees to register new active ingredients not listed in the Registration Division 2003 Work Plan of the Office of Pesticide Programs. The Pesticide Registration Improvement Renewal Act (commonly referred to as PRIA II) extended the authority to collect pesticide registration service fees through FY 2012. PRIA II became effective October 1, 2007. The PRIA Fund is accounted for under Treasury symbol number 68X5374.

PRIA may charge some administrative costs directly to the fund and charge the remainder of the administrative costs to Agency-wide appropriations. Costs funded by Agency-wide appropriations for FYs 2010 and 2009 were $37,256 thousand and $49,215 thousand, respectively. This amount was included as Income from Other Appropriations on the Statement of Changes in Net Position and as Expenses from Other Appropriations on the Statement of Net Cost for FYs 2010 and 2009.

B. Basis of Presentation

These financial statements have been prepared to report the financial position and results of operations of the Environmental Protection Agency (EPA) for the Pesticide Registration Fund (PRIA) as required by the Chief Financial Officers Act of 1990 and the Pesticide Registration Improvement Act (PRIA) of 2003. In the prior years, pesticide registration was included in the FIFRA financial statements. The reports have been prepared from the books and records of EPA in accordance with Office of Management and Budget (OMB) Circular A-136 *Financial Reporting Requirements,* and EPA's accounting policies which are summarized in this note.

These statements are therefore different from the financial reports also prepared by EPA pursuant to OMB directives that are used to monitor and control EPA's use of budgetary resources. The balances in these reports have been updated from the EPA consolidated financial statements to reflect the use of FY 2010 cost factors for calculating imputed costs for Federal civilian benefits programs. These updates impact the Balance Sheet, Statement of Net Cost, and Statement of Changes in Net Position.

C. Budgets and Budgetary Accounting

Funding for PRIA is provided by fees collected from industry to offset costs incurred by EPA in carrying out these programs. Each year EPA submits an apportionment request to OMB based on the anticipated collections of industry fees.

D. Basis of Accounting

Generally Accepted Accounting Principles (GAAP) for Federal entities is the standard prescribed by the Federal Accounting Standards Advisory Board (FASAB), which is the official standard setting body for the federal government. The financial statements are prepared in accordance with GAAP for federal entities.

Transactions are recorded on an accrual accounting basis and a budgetary basis. Under the accrual method, revenues are recognized when earned and expenses are recognized when a liability is incurred, without regard to receipt or payment of cash. Budgetary accounting facilitates compliance with legal constraints and controls over the use of Federal funds. All interfund balances and transactions have been eliminated.

E. Revenues and Other Financing Sources

For FYs 2010 and 2009, PRIA received funding from fees collected from registrants requesting pesticide registrations. For FYs 2010 and 2009, revenues were recognized from fee collections to the extent that expenses are incurred during the fiscal year.

F. Funds with the Treasury

The PRIA fund deposits receipts and processes disbursements through its operating account maintained at the U.S. Department of the Treasury.

G. Investments in U. S. Government Securities

Investments in U. S. government securities are maintained by Treasury and are reported at amortized cost net of unamortized discounts. Discounts are amortized over the term of the investments and reported as interest income. FIFRA holds the investments to maturity, unless needed to finance operations of the fund. No provision is made for unrealized gains or losses on these securities because, in the majority of cases, they are held to maturity.

H. General Property, Plant and Equipment

Purchases of EPA-held personal equipment are capitalized if the equipment is valued at $25 thousand or more and has an estimated useful life of at least two years. Depreciation is taken on a basic straight-line method over the specific asset's useful life, ranging from two to15 years. EPA shows property, plant and equipment at net of depreciation on its audited financial statements.

All funds (except for the Working Capital Fund) capitalize software if those investments are considered Capital Planning and Investment Control (CPIC) or CPIC Lite systems with the provisions of SFFAS No. 10, "Accounting for Internal Use Software." Once software enters the production life cycle phase, it is depreciated using the straight-line method over the specific asset's useful life ranging from two to 10 years.

I. Liabilities

Liabilities represent the amount of monies or other resources that are likely to be paid by the Agency as the result of an Agency transaction or event that has already occurred and can be reasonably estimated. However, no liability can be paid by the Agency without an appropriation or other collections. Liabilities for which an appropriation has not been enacted are classified as unfunded liabilities and there is no certainty that the appropriations will be enacted. For PRIA, liabilities are liquidated from fee receipts, since PRIA receives no appropriation. Liabilities of the Agency arising from anything other than contracts can be abrogated by the Government acting in its sovereign capacity.

J. Accrued Unfunded Annual Leave

Annual, sick and other leave is expensed as taken during the fiscal year. Sick leave earned but not taken is not accrued as a liability. Annual leave earned but not taken as of the end of the fiscal year is accrued as an unfunded liability. Accrued unfunded annual leave is included in the Balance Sheet as a component of "Payroll and Benefits Payable."

K. Retirement Plan

There are two primary retirement systems for Federal employees. Employees hired prior to January 1, 1987, may participate in the Civil Service Retirement System (CSRS). On January 1, 1984, the Federal Employees Retirement System (FERS) went into effect pursuant to Public Law 99-335. Most employees hired after December 31, 1983, are automatically covered by FERS and Social Security. Employees hired prior to January 1, 1984, elected to either join FERS and Social Security or remain in CSRS. A primary feature of FERS is that it offers a savings plan to which the Agency automatically contributes one percent of pay and matches any employee contributions up to an additional four percent of pay. The Agency also contributes the employer's matching share for Social Security.

With the issuance of SFFAS No. 5, "Accounting for Liabilities of the Federal Government," accounting and reporting standards were established for liabilities relating to the federal employee benefit programs (Retirement, Health Benefits, and Life Insurance). SFFAS No. 5 requires that the employing agencies recognize the cost of pensions and other retirement benefits during their employees' active years of service. SFFAS No. 5 requires that the Office of Personnel Management (OPM), as administrator of the CSRS and FERS, the Federal Employees Health Benefits Program, and the Federal Employees Group Life Insurance Program, provide federal agencies with the actuarial cost factors to compute the liability for each program.

L.   Offsetting Receipts

Beginning in FY 2007 OMB Circular A-136, *Financial Reporting Requirements,* requires that the amount of distributed offsetting receipts reported in the Statement of Budgetary Resources (SBR) should equal the amount recorded as offsetting receipts by the Department of the Treasury (Treasury). Pesticide Registration Fees collected under PRIA are considered to be offsetting receipts by Treasury.

M. Use of Estimates

The preparation of financial statements requires management to make certain estimates and assumptions that affect the reported amounts of assets and liabilities and the reported amounts of revenue and expenses during the reporting period. Actual results could differ from those estimates.

Note 2. Fund Balance with Treasury

		FY 2010	FY 2009
Revolving Funds:	Entity Assets	$ 15,094	$ 15,140

Note 3. Other Assets

Other Assets consist of advances for Interagency Agreements.

Note 4. General Property, Plant and Equipment

General property, plant and equipment consists of EPA-Held personal property and software in development.

As of September 30, 2010 and 2009, General Property, Plant and Equipment consist of the following:

	FY 2010			FY 2009		
	Acquisition Value	Accumulated Depreciation	Net Book Value	Acquisition Value	Accumulated Depreciation	Net Book Value
EPA-Held Equipment	$ 446	$ (239)	$ 207	$ 319	$ (238)	$ 81
Software	4,238	-	4,238	3,562	-	3,562
Total	**$ 4,684**	**$ (239)**	**$ 4,445**	**$ 3,881**	**$ (238)**	**$ 3,643**

Note 5. Other Liabilities

For FYs 2010 and 2009, Payroll and Benefits Payable, non-federal, are presented on a separate line of the Balance Sheet and in a separate footnote (see Note 6).

	FY 2010	FY 2009
Other Intragovernmental Liabilities - Covered by Budgetary Resources		
Employer Contributions - Payroll	$ 21	$ 79
Total	**$ 21**	**$ 79**
Other Non-Federal Liabilities - Covered by Budgetary Resources		
Advances from Non-Federal Entities	$ 14,088	$ 13,421
Total	**$ 14,088**	**$ 13,421**

Note 6. Payroll and Benefits Payable, Non-Federal:

	FY 2010		FY 2009	
Covered by Budgetary Resources				
Accrued Payroll Payable to Employees	$	61	$	227
Withholdings Payable		29		124
Thrift Savings Plan Benefits Payable		3		12
Total	$	**93**	$	**363**
Not Covered by Budgetary Resources				
Unfunded Annual Leave	$	146	$	593
Total	$	**146**	$	**593**

At various periods throughout FYs 2010 and 2009 employees with their associated payroll costs were transferred from the fund to the Environmental Programs and Management (EPM) appropriation. (See graph in Note 7 below showing trend of hours charged per month to the PRIA Fund for FYs 2010 and 2009.) These employees were transferred in order to keep PRIA's obligations and disbursements within budgetary limits.

This process has led to variations between the year-end liabilities of FYs 2010 and 2009. The liabilities covered by budgetary resources (both intragovernmental and non-Federal) represent unpaid payroll and benefits at year-end. For FY 2010 Pay Period 26; 18 employees charged to PRIA part of their salary and benefits. As of September 30, 2010, these liabilities were $21 thousand and $93 thousand for employer contributions and accrued funded payroll and benefits as compared to FY 2009's balances of $79 thousand and $363 thousand, respectively.

In contrast, the unfunded annual leave liability is a longer term liability than the funded liabilities. At various periods throughout FYs 2010 and FY 2009, approximately 144 and 173 employees, respectively, in total have been under PRIA's accountability. As of September 30, 2010 and 2009 liability balances for unfunded annual leave were accrued to cover these employees for a total of $146 thousand and $593 thousand, respectively.

Note 7. Income and Expenses from Other Appropriations:

The Statement of Net Cost reports program costs that include the full costs of the program outputs and consist of the direct costs and all other costs that can be directly traced, assigned on a cause and effect basis, or reasonably allocated to program outputs.

During FYs 2010 and 2009, EPA had two appropriations which funded a variety of programmatic and non-programmatic activities across the Agency, subject to statutory requirements. The EPM appropriation was created to fund personnel compensation and benefits, travel, procurement, and contract activities. Transfers of employees from PRIA to EPM at various times during FYs 2010 and 2009 (see Note 6 above) resulted in an increase in payroll expenses in EPM, and these costs financed by EPM are reflected as an increase in the Expenses from Other Appropriations on the Statement of Net Cost. The increased financing from EPM is reported on the Statement of Changes in Net Position as Income from Other Appropriations.

In terms of hours charged to PRIA each month, the transfers of employees and their associated costs during FYs 2010 and 2009 are shown below. Note that a decrease in hours charged to PRIA normally signifies an increase in EPM's payroll costs, and vice versa.

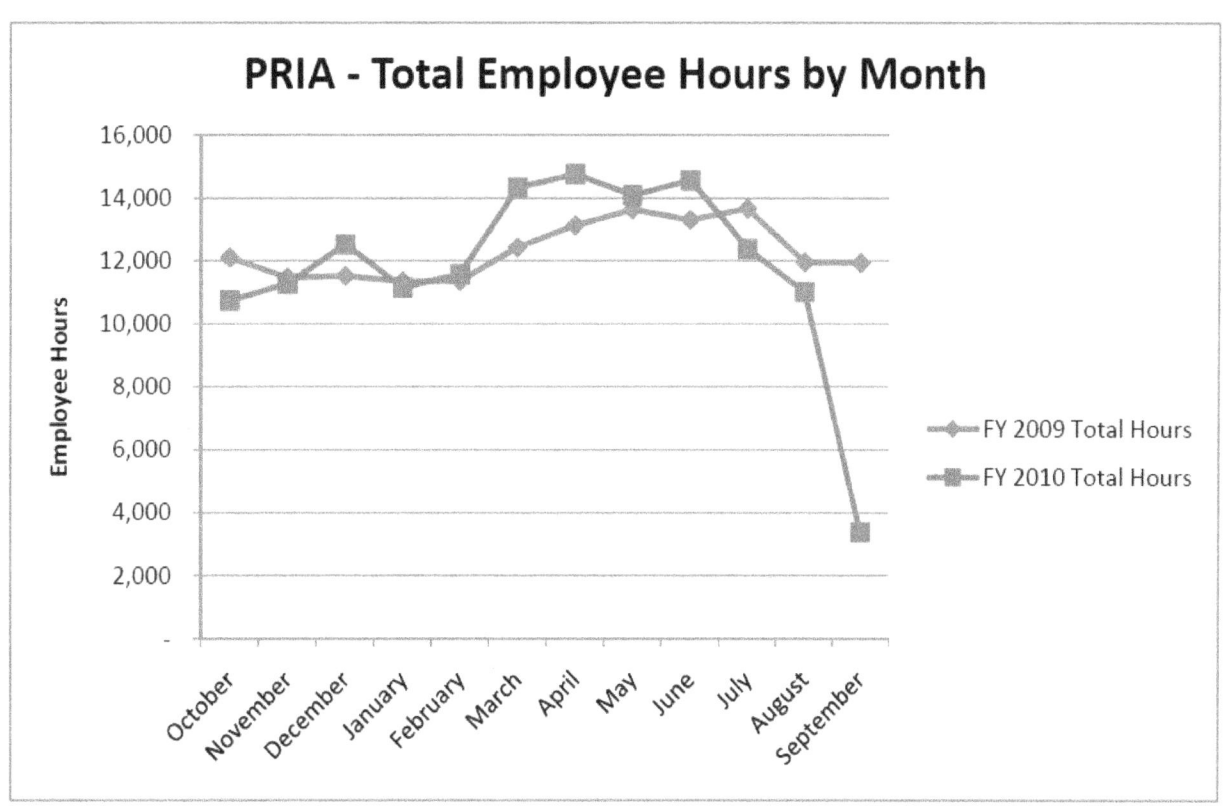

EPM costs related to PRIA are allocated based on specific EPM program codes which have been designated for Pesticide registration activities. As illustrated below, there is no impact on PRIA's Statement of Net Position.

	Income From Other Appropriations	Expenses From Other Appropriations	Net Effect
FY 2010	$ 37,256	$ 37,256	$ 0
FY 2009	$ 49,215	$ 49,215	$ 0

Note 8. *Exchange Revenues, Statement of Net Cost*

For FYs 2010 and 2009, the exchange revenues reported on the Statement of Net Cost consists of non-Federal amounts.

Note 9. *Intragovernmental Costs and Exchange Revenue*

	FY 2010	FY 2009
COSTS:		
Intragovernmental	$ 2,730	$ 2,776
With the Public	14,260	13,538
Expenses from Other Appropriations	37,256	49,215
Total Costs	$ 54,246	$ 65,529
REVENUE:		
With the Public	17,885	17,850
Total Revenue	$ 17,885	$ 17,850
NET COST OF OPERATIONS	**$ 36,361**	**$ 47,679**

Intragovernmental costs relate to the source of the goods or services not the classification of the related revenue.

Note 10. *Reconciliation of Net Cost of Operations to Budget (formerly the Statement of Financing)*

	FY 2010	FY 2009
RESOURCES USED TO FINANCE ACTIVITIES:		
Budgetary Resources Obligated		
Obligations Incurred	$ 18,147	$ 18,211
Less: Spending Authority from Offsetting Collections and Recoveries	(3)	(321)
Obligations, Net of Offsetting Collections	$ 18,144	$ 17,890
Less: Offsetting Receipts (Note 1 Section L)	(18,557)	(15,833)
Net Obligations	(413)	2,057
Other Resources		
Imputed Financing Sources	$ 355	$ 12
Income from Other Appropriations (Note 7)	37,256	49,215
Net Other Resources Used to Finance Activities	$ 37,611	$ 49,227
Total Resources Used To Finance Activities	$ 37,198	$ 51,284
RESOURCES USED TO FINANCE ITEMS		
NOT PART OF NET COST OF OPERATIONS		
Change in Budgetary Resources Obligated	$ (261)	$ (38)
Resources that Fund Prior Periods Expenses	(446)	-
Offsetting Receipts Not Affecting Net Cost (Note 1 Section L)	18,557	15,833
Resources that Finance Asset Acquistion	(803)	(1,684)
Total Resources Used to Finance Items Not		
Part of the Net Cost of Operations	$ 17,047	$ 14,111
Total Resources Used to Finance the Net		
Cost of Operations	$ 54,245	$ 65,395
COMPONENTS OF NET COST OF OPERATIONS		
THAT WILL NOT REQUIRE OR GENERATE		
RESOURCES IN THE CURRENT PERIOD		
Components Requiring or Generating Resources in Future Periods:		
Increase in Annual Leave Liability	$ -	$ 98
Increase in Public Exchange Revenue Receivable	(17,885)	(17,850)
Total Components of Net Cost of Operations that		
Requires or Generates Resources in the Future	$ (17,885)	$ (17,752)
Components Not Requiring/Generating Resources:		
Depreciation and Amortization	1	36
Total components of Net cost of Operations that Will Not Require or Generate Resources	1	36
Total components of Net cost of Operations that Will Not Require		
or Generate Resources in the Current Period	(17,884)	(17,716)
Net Cost of Operations	$ 36,361	$ 47,679

Distribution

Office of the Administrator
Chief Financial Officer
Assistant Administrator for Chemical Safety and Pollution Prevention
Assistant Administrator for Administration and Resources Management
Deputy Chief Financial Officer
Agency Followup Coordinator
General Counsel
Associate Administrator for Congressional and Intragovernmental Relations
Associate Administrator for External Affairs and Environmental Information
Director, Office of Pesticide Programs, Office of Chemical Safety and Pollution Prevention
Deputy Director, Office of Pesticide Programs, Office of Chemical Safety and Pollution Prevention
Senior Advisor, PRIA Implementation, Office of Pesticide Programs, Office of Chemical Safety
        and Pollution Prevention
Acting Director, Biopesticides and Pollution Prevention Division, Office of Pesticide Programs,
        Office of Chemical Safety and Pollution Prevention
Director, Pesticide Re-Evaluation Division, Office of Pesticide Programs, Office of Chemical
        Safety and Pollution Prevention
Director, Registration Division, Office of Pesticide Programs, Office of Chemical Safety and
        Pollution Prevention
Director, Antimicrobials Division, Office of Pesticide Programs, Office of Chemical Safety and
        Pollution Prevention
Director, Information Technology and Resources Management Division, Office of Pesticide
        Programs, Office of Chemical Safety and Pollution Prevention
Director, Office of Human Resources, Office of Administration and Resources Management
Director, Office of Financial Management, Office of the Chief Financial Officer
Director, Office of Financial Services, Office of the Chief Financial Officer
Director, Reporting and Analysis Staff, Office of the Chief Financial Officer
Director, Financial Policy and Planning Staff, Office of the Chief Financial Officer
Director, Research Triangle Park Finance Center, Office of the Chief Financial Officer
Director, Cincinnati Finance Center, Office of the Chief Financial Officer
Director, Las Vegas Finance Center, Office of the Chief Financial Officer
Director, Payroll Management and Outreach Staff, Office of Financial Services,
        Office of the Chief Financial Officer
Staff Director, Accountability and Control Staff, Office of Financial Services, Office of the
        Chief Financial Officer
Audit Followup Coordinator, Office of the Chief Financial Officer
Audit Followup Coordinator, Office of Chemical Safety and Pollution Prevention
Audit Followup Coordinator, Office of Administration and Resources Management
PRIA Audit Coordinator, Office of Pesticide Programs, Office of Chemical Safety and
        Pollution Prevention

www.ingramcontent.com/pod-product-compliance
Lightning Source LLC
Chambersburg PA
CBHW081802280526
45789CB00008B/2964